Did You Know That's Not My Name?

Tall

Big

short

Quick

Poor

Rich

Small

Smart

Written by Diana T. Durso

Illustrated by Jill M. Bentz

AuthorHouse™
1663 Liberty Drive
Bloomington, IN 47403
www.authorhouse.com
Phone: 833-262-8899

Because of the dynamic nature of the Internet, any web addresses or links contained in this book may have changed
since publication and may no longer be valid. The views expressed in this work are solely those of the author and do not
necessarily reflect the views of the publisher, and the publisher hereby disclaims any responsibility for them.

Any people depicted in stock imagery provided by Getty Images are models,
and such images are being used for illustrative purposes only.
Certain stock imagery © Getty Images.

This book is printed on acid-free paper.

ISBN: 978-1-4389-3182-1 (sc)

Print information available on the last page.

Published by AuthorHouse 11/19/2022

authorHOUSE®

Did You Know That's Not My Name?

Tall

Big

short

Quick

Poor

Rich

Small

Smart

slow

Written by: Diana T. Durso

Illustrated by: Jill M. Bentz

About the Book

This is a delightful rhyming story, which is easy reading for children of all ages.

The lessons taught in this story are invaluable. They encourage children to believe in themselves and embrace their unique qualities. It also teaches children to use their voice to stand up for themselves against put downs and teasing, in order to overcome their challenges.

Dedication

I would like to dedicate this book in loving memory of my father, Richard S. Porto. He would be proud of the lessons this story teaches of strength, confidence, and believing in oneself. Thanks Dad!

Acknowledgments

I first need to thank my husband, Ray, for encouraging me to pursue my dream of writing and his much needed guidance along the way, as well as, my children Gennaro, Gianna, and Alexa Rae. I want to thank my dear colleague and friend Jill Bentz, the illustrator of this story, who truly brought my ideas to life with her beautiful pictures! She believed in me and my story which means the world to me. Thank you to Joseph P. Bottini for his guidance on how to publish a book. Special thanks to my teacher friends Kathy Downey, Lisa Dellaposta, and Sharon Belfield for their support and advice. Also, kudos to my brother in law, Vinny Pastorella, who assisted me with the technical preparation. Thank you to family and friends for your continued support. Finally, thank you to the students of the class of 2007-2008 who truly inspired me to write this story!

Did you know that's not my name?

My name is really
Mary Jane.

Some kids call me big...

Others call me small...

Then there are those who
don't see me at all.

I may be big...
I may be small...
I know I am here...
I can see them all!

Did you know that's not my name?

Don't you know I have a brain?
I want you to call me by my name...
That name is really Mary Jane.

Some kids call me short...

Others call me tall ...

I may be short...
I may be tall...
I know I am here...
I will tell them all!

Don't you know I have a brain?
I want you to call me by my name...
That name is really Mary Jane.

Some kids call me rich...

Others call me poor...

Then there are those who won't sit near me anymore.

I may be rich...
I may be poor...
I know I am here...
I will still soar!

Did you know that's
not my name?

Don't you know I have a brain?
I want you to call me by my name...
That name is really Mary Jane.

Others call me quick...

Then there are those who don't want me in their clique.

Did you know
that's not my
name?

Don't you know I have a brain?
I want you to call me by my name...
That name is really Mary Jane.

Some kids call me dumb...

Others call me smart...

Then there are those who don't like me from the start.

I'm big!
I'm small!
I'm ten feet tall!

I'm short!
I'm tall!
I'm like a brick wall!

I'm slow!
I'm quick!
My skin is thick!

I'm rich!
I'm poor!
I am so much more!

Now you know I have a name.

Now you know I have a brain.

I want you to call me by this name...

And that name is ONLY Mary Jane!

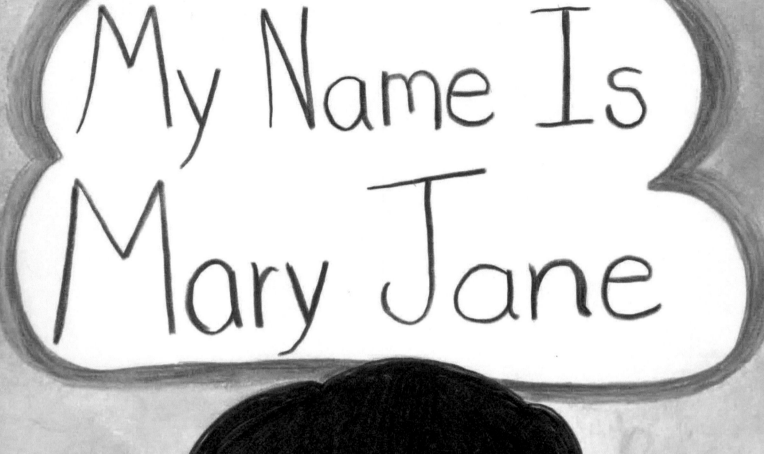

About the Author

Diana Durso lives in Utica, New York. She is a School Social Worker currently working with elementary age students grades kindergarten through five.

She is an advocate for children promoting self-confidence and enhancing self-esteem. She encourages children that their voice is strong and can be heard.

Diana is married with three children ages 10, 7, and 3. She was inspired by her children and her students to begin the process of writing her first children's story!

Printed in the United States
by Baker & Taylor Publisher Services